THE CIRCLE OF TOTEMS

Peggy Shumaker

The Circle of Totems

University of Pittsburgh Press

For my family

Published by the University of Pittsburgh Press, Pittsburgh, Pa. 15260
Copyright © 1988, Peggy Shumaker
All rights reserved
Feffer and Simons, Inc., London
Manufactured in the United States of America

Library of Congress Cataloging in Publication Data
Shumaker, Peggy, 1952–
    The circle of totems / Peggy Shumaker.
        p.   cm. — (Pitt poetry series)
    ISBN 0-8229-3578-3.   ISBN 0-8229-5402-8 (pbk.)
    I. Title. II. Series.
PS3569.H778C5 1988
811'.54—dc 19   87-25189
                                              CIP

Many thanks to the editors and publishers of the journals in which these poems first appeared: *Black Warrior Review* ("The Circle of Totems"); *Colorado Review* ("Owl/ Beating"); *5 AM* ("Cinco de Mayo" and "How, as in Hopscotch, Heaven Is Round"); *Hayden's Ferry Review* ("Newlywed," "The Waitress's Kid," and "The Cousin on Holiday"); *Heartland* ("The Circle of Totems," "On the Way Back, He Walks Behind," "Shepherds," and "Why Scorpions Don't Fly"); *Iowa Woman* ("Lost Watch"); *MSS* ("After Talking to My Husband's Lover"); *Nebraska Review* ("Matisse's Antoinette" and "Genealogies"); *New Delta Review* ("Why Scorpions Don't Fly"); *North American Review* ("Blue Ridge Reservoir"); *Permafrost* ("Dockside, Bahia, Carnaval," "Blue Apples," and "Where Mountains Have No Names"); *Poetry Northwest* ("Turned Wood"); *Prairie Schooner* ("First Thing in the Morning, Eclairs, Lightning," "Pastoral: Squash and Rice," and "Vespers"); and *Prickly Pear* ("The Ornithologists' Son" and "Visitation").

The author would like to thank the College of Arts and Letters at Old Dominion University for a faculty research grant.

The publication of this book is supported by grants from the National Endowment for the Arts in Washington, D.C., a Federal agency, and the Pennsylvania Council on the Arts.

But blue will swallow black like a bell swallows silence "to echo a grief that is hardly human." Because blue contracts, retreats, it is the color of transcendence, leading us away in pursuit of the infinite.

—William Gass, *On Being Blue*

Contents

Contents

III

I

"For nothing can be sole or whole
That has not been rent."
—W. B. Yeats, "Crazy Jane
Talks with the Bishop"

Newlywed

It was the morning Vixen
broke through the fence—shouldered over
the splintered cedar
she'd clawed loose and bolted
down the arroyo and into the cholla.

My mouth had dried in the night. My tongue
reached for the corners, smaller now and hard,
and tried to moisten them. I was ashamed
how I might smell to you,
though you were happy to see me then
in the first light.

I let you watch me sleep.
I was still lost
in the dream of adobe houses melting
without roofs—a wide open
blank white sky
smothering all the world.
I shuddered, jerking fully to sleep,
and you understood that
as a sign of my waking,
laid a hand on my waist.

You wore on the back of your hand
a rare but serviceable leather.
I held my mouth to your broken places.

When I rose to wash the tight dried smears
from my thighs, you found her
whimpering at the sliding
door, her prodigal muzzle
bearded with fine white spines.

How, as in Hopscotch, Heaven Is Round

Even as she scoops onto her tongue
oily mouthfuls of windfall avocado,
she has become completely two
people. She watches herself behaving

like some deranged saint, blessing
the dirt clods, hears her own voice—
raspy leaves of Carolina tobacco
opening. This addled girl steps through
tender as spread asphalt, and perspiring
slightly. The beaded child has been
drinking under a clean moon.

How far advanced the trees are!
In the big house the cook's boy
cuts a snowflake from notebook paper.
She arranges it, careful to the edges,
powders her spring-back spicecake.

There should be songs for this,
for the girl whose bones have turned
to water between deep furrows,
the girl who circles toward home
through the drying sheds, so the aroma
of her love's thigh should lose itself there
among the leaves, brittle and addictive.

Songs, for the cook
who wears the same clothes for laughing
or crying, the cook who can feel
around her right nipple
the odd shape of her boy's mouth, years ago,
a huge eyelid, clamping down . . .

A song for the avocado woman
holding her own, spiraling,
a rolled-up tapestry, pattern-side in,
sprinkled with pepper
against the moths.

Dockside, Bahia, Carnaval

The tall-necked bottles stood watch while they touched her, while they got up from their places at other tables or along the curb and crowded in till her air was too small—they pressed in hips first, these dark men who had always before half-hidden their faces behind hunched shoulders, or kept their eyes deep under lashes. But now those eyes lashed out over the open-mouthed bottles where they'd drunk this courage, and their fingers tested her belly, tenderly at first as they would a rising loaf of sweetbread, then poking harder because she closed her eyes to the panic.

If he had cared for her, Vadinho could have pulled her back through the dockworkers, past the waiters and off-duty cabdrivers through the small clutch of whores smoking black cigarettes and balancing on tall boots, he could have lifted her backwards bodily to a place where she could breathe, some gutter full of confetti and broken glass. Vadinho's thick palm, the one that fit perfectly around the handle of the machete that hacked open coconuts with a single clout, hand that crushed walnut shells without cracking the dusty meats inside, fingers that held the robber Clemente fast by gouging out one eye, that hand, that black hand singed her midriff. Its heat stole the rest of her breath and she cried, "Leave me!" But Vadinho hissed over her shoulder, "Puta branca, branca, branca."

Pastoral: Squash and Rice

Two halves of lemon
squeezed out for toddies
Eden's mother tosses
to the molting hens.

Wet tatters blacken
along the rims
of the rinds: grimy mouths
of her weaker students
outlined in last night's supper—
unwashed carrots
yanked after dusk.

Her new husband, a doubtful plumber
this time, sloshes the last inch
of Wild Turkey, calling, "How many ways
we got to split this?"

The redtail regards her,
spreads its talons for a better grip,
gouging the arthritic arms of blue juniper
masking the landlord's rammed-earth walls.

For fruit leather,
for a cinnamon tortilla,
her daughter meows.
The butcher knife splits
orange bark off the butternut,
minces a half moon of garlic
for the rice.

What can she hear with her wrists
pressed into her temples?
The lemon water
nearly has boiled away.

On the screenporch
one eggplant has begun
going bad:

her grandmother's breast
left like this,
spongy and moonlit, its dry nipple
hardening as it cooled . . .

First Thing in the Morning, Eclairs, Lightning

All night, the sky in frenzy.

Before the restless
town has stretched and
coughed, the baker's
dough has risen, browned,
cooled, then shaken
in perfect slices between steel
blades. All the delicious
emptinesses impaled with
custard or cream
present themselves on paper
doilies like second,
better thoughts.

His deft
palm pats sliced
almonds against
the sheer face
of a triple
rum cake.

Back home, his obese
dusty-eyed
daughter is calling
socorro, socorro, the walker
somehow through the flash-ripped
night has strayed
simpering in its rubber
shoes too far
from her
unsprung bed.

Almond, almond, almond—
in the whipped fragile
middle of a batch of royal
icing, he reads her lips.

He will leave work swearing
violently to tend her
because too much,
how he loves
her, is too much.

The Cousin on Holiday

Lise-Marie spread boysenberry
preserves on my knees and licked
them. She said she must
till the butterscotch tab
between my back teeth
disappeared completely.
But the parents drove home
a day early from Boston.
Of course, they sacked
poor Lise-Marie
immediately. Papa drew me
off her lap, smoothed my smeared
skirt, then shoved me
into the bath. There was great shouting,
breaking jars, and I longed
to soothe Lise-Marie with the tips
of my braids.

All the way here,
backseat to Colorado,
crouching, watching their necks
stiffen. I would not let them
touch me. I brought
only the too-strong sachet
Lise-Marie dried
secretly. . . . When the time came,
I signed
where the chipper aide
pointed. Then she took my violent
fragrance, for good, away.

The matron allows me
run of the grounds, if only
I'll keep my smock
buttoned. It's coarse,
Lise-Marie, and gray, with the poorest
excuse for sleeves. At dusk
I lower a long-handled
dipper into the radium springs.
I empty it in my lap.
Along the path, forced water
splays upward in a silver cone.
They expect snow soon.
No one mentions
my going home.

Owl / Beating

When the headlights bored through
we saw differently, not more.
The glow between the saguaro's spines.
Quick glint—
unlikely moisture on the hardpan
jeep trail—yards down
we marked it, some living thing
murmuring in unreliable light.
Growing feathers
as we stepped
softly toward it.
Two cupped hands
full of terror,
even as we smoothed
the shirred edges, cooed echoes
to the gurgles of strangled
owl language. Brushed out
a hollow in the velvet
mesquite. Restored
the heart to its place,
nearer the sky.

Shepherds

Smoke from one chimney
testifies miles down
across Hart Prairie and past the aspen:
the freeway twists that way.

We've taken ungraded trails
far off, wanting this bed
of pine slash and lava,
this supper of warm gouda
wedged from red wax.

At pure dark, stars move over
to make room for the moon.
Our larger eyes grow
accustomed to such light.

In thin air, anything
is possible—even my fingers
teasing your peppered beard,
the lovely hollow shepherding
of long devotion.

From a distance, the tin snips
of Basque shepherds chink—
bells, new bells,
they're fastening on red bells.

On the Way Back, He Walks Behind

As if they had warmed a place days ago,
cows hunker down, furry boulders
poking through frozen snow.

A hauled-back canteen hammers through
stained isinglass topping the runoff.
One waterproof toe holds it under.

Apart from the pulling and hauling,
this space, this visible breath—
a game of statues and attitudes:

the torso of the man I will marry,
worthy to be naked, knotted and sailing,
heaves the ax into standing deadwood.

Trail mix balanced in my shivering palm
he collects with plush lips onto his tongue.
Pocket knife, tortillas, smoky links, cheese—

his touch—like bumping the lit end
of a stranger's cigarette—
fire in his mouth, his teeth glinting—

In the season of first columbine
I bury his body. His fire
comes back green. Hard muscles

vicious with grace.

Water Island

We were suffering the last days
of a lost good marriage.
Could not afford a single
harsh word. I left early
to swim a new spot.

Skittery pebbles
sloped off, a gradual decline
into clarity. I spit in my mask,
sucked long narrow breaths
through the curved tube.
Tried floating too soon, scraped
one breast against a shell ridge.

A few straightlegged strums and pushed
water pushed me into the world beyond sound—
silent duststorms of fish, brain coral
tangled into and into itself.

I followed a clown fish, a kissing fish,
two angels. Heard steel drums breaking joy
into little pieces and handing it
back to us.

When my breaths gave out, I arced
back to the pier. Two sailboats
had lowered their blow-up rafts
blocking the ladder. Under the mossy
roof pressing down, I swam between pilings
to the end of the dock, unwilling to walk out
now that people were up and waving.

Palms flat on the weathered planks,
I scissored twice and breached,
elbow-heaving onto a solid surface.

On the way up my thighs grazed
the coated pole. Rolling,
I watched the burns begin to blister.
Fire coral!

Long as I didn't move
I could stand it, but I had to
walk back. All the way
up the beach people called out
remedies.

After Talking to My Husband's Lover

When I take off my dress
I no longer have a secret
place left in me.

Why Scorpions Don't Fly

Elena was instructed early on to pray
for a better temper.
She listened so hard for an answer
she heard chicken bones

dissolve inside the cat.
Handy punishment, silence:
it took her thirty years
to figure out

she wasn't guilty enough
to be forgiven so much.
She held back, beyond all promises—
suffered the false meekness

of an anger that does not know
its own name. She knew the language
which has no word for hunger,
for every word is hunger.

All her days people watched
as if she were an eclipse—
never risking a hard look
straight at her. Until the morning

she surfaced clear as flame grain
flaring from a nozzle-sprayed
redwood burl. Her peacock eyes
sambaed in the face of a woman

who has dreamed of a stranger.
His hands have yet to reach inside her,
but his tongue has cupped the silver drop
hesitating on her wishbone.

His mouth confirms her suspicion:
curiosity is braver than rage.
Then she could set aside her poison—
por eso no vuela el alacrán.

19

Matisse's Antoinette

Because they are truly her friends, they leave her
tasting salt in her dreams, salt and green lemons.
Cool porcelain, a windowsill, vanilla and wax.
        Her friends leave her
flowers, and tied to the flowers, a note
scratched on butcher paper. Blue-black gentian
folded in a green waxed cone. Their last
cut hours sweated out formally, each stem
arranged in the swirl-glazed tureen.

In the bath, she stretches full-length—
two bruised red peonies surface.
Because she did not love him, she allowed
one young man to stroke the sleek slope
of her hip, wondering what he would find
to possess, what she had
to parcel, what one
needs must conserve, always. How little
it has to do with the body.

Vespers

In the failing light
our crumpled fastback high-stepped
over ruts and gullies
back toward El Camino del Cerro.
Lights of the city
trickled up the foothills—
Rincon, Catalina, Tortolita, Tucson.
Our husky tongues cracked,
jojoba beans in dusty jackets.
Hiking, we'd left the rest
of a potluck potato salad
ripening on the back seat.
Someone we never saw,
never heard, left the bowl
and spoon and made his way on.

We left the headlights off
long as we could, savoring
dusk's long coming.
Fragrance of creosote.
Cheap wine and a profound
good will toward one another.
No sense
that there could be
an end to this.

II

And the color, the overcast blue
Of the air, in which the blue guitar

Is a form, described but difficult,
And I am merely a shadow hunched

Above the arrowy, still strings,
the maker of a thing yet to be made

—Wallace Stevens, "The Man with the Blue Guitar"

Sugarbird, Hiding

The ferryboat's wake
has taken morning to St. Thomas.

Though her hair is short,
the woman left behind

shakes her head in the sun.
She hides now,

a sugarbird
liquid between leaves,

glides like oiled fingers
over the temples of her lover.

In the hanging gardens
she finds a likeness

of a self she once imagined—
Nike, balanced, one wing open,

bending to remove her sandal.
Tall ships slice the immediate water.

The tuned delicacy of the tendons
in her neck would tempt a guitarist

but no one listens now, no one
looks on as she loosens her clothing,

dropping each piece in a path behind her.
She breaks the clear mosaic of the water.

On her chest two rose windows harden,
a decent politeness,

a saying *hello*. A deaf man
once held her hand too long

then explained *I could hear your heartbeat
in my palm*. She swims face down,

her breath piped in,
singing underwater, humming

How much we have to forgive . . .
till the lace-grained sun insists

with a constant thud
at the back of the head

Come back, come . . .
in a secret life

you can never tell if you're happy.
In her room, at this moment

her husband and his sister
search her luggage.

They insist she come to dinner
with a pleasant face.

Visitation

(for my sister)

The lover you cannot dream of
will be with you tonight,
entering like a thief softly forcing a door.
He has returned to teach you what the brave
stay too busy to believe.

With a juggler's unconcern, he tosses you
into a bus headed for Las Vegas.
It's air conditioned, but you're hot
for him anyway. The woman across the aisle
fingerspells something about oranges
or scruples, you can't tell which.

Your lover has saved for months
to take you here, and so examines your face
for appropriately copious pleasure—
rhinestones? —sequins? How about it?
You want to be delirious for him,
but manage only a faint resemblance
to the pale tallow left under candlecrowns
on Nazarene altars.
You cringe like a child on stage,
terrified of the crack in the curtain,
anxious that the light will reach in
to tug at her nipples, fondle her
little half-apricots in front
of everybody, until in grim ecstasy
she wets herself.
You assume in all humility
the absent shape of your lover's feet.

So you will lie down
not inside the burning kiln
reserved for shapes of use or ornament,
but on top, like the monsters
children place there for luck, insurance,

27

so jars they've patted out themselves
may lift free glowing and whole, tongs
rolling them in sawdust till raku cracks
splinter across glazed faces.

Don't misunderstand—
when your face burns, ashamed
and wild
as the unfilled places
on maps of Africa, your lover
will crumple on the kitchen tile.
By then you will have become for him
a woman made wholly of light.
You'll place your ear against his chest,
all the guidebooks recommend . . .
wanting at least the heart's
specious alibi, the rhythm

> *Listen for the sound of a cellar*
> *when the key is lost.*

The Ornithologists' Son

Because he'd grown up
in an armed compound
reserved for birds,
Fernandez had eyes
like ermine leaping
at cardinals just beyond
their jaws' clasp.
Those restless eyes
and red long johns
unbuttoned at the chin,
chest of a tastebud's ocean.

Marion's homemade Irish cream
slipped down his gullet
till he burbled like Liam's chickens
startled in their wire corral.
Over the drowsy St. Bernards
his wallet flipped automatically
open to the nude photo
of his three year old.

That's why later I startled awake—
rough bootsteps
scraping the unplaned
lumber of the loft
where I'd crawled early
between the glacial layers
of the bag I'd fill
with my own body's warming.
His drunken goodnight
settled halfway on my mouth,
his fingers gliding down my shape as if
I were a half-made dulcimer,
ready for pearling. The low roof
listened in: his voice
filled with mustache wax

29

took the nine girlfriends
before he was married
only as better proof
of his guitar-string fidelity.
He talked all night
about home, Jill, about the ring
he didn't wear.

Next morning he pressed me
snug against the stove
where I stood fixing soup
and whispered over my shoulder
into my ear—*You know I wanted
you, hard, last night.*
And it was perfectly pleasant,
the milky onion, the broth,
the stripped turkey carcass,
his noticeable virtue
pressing against me.

Cinco de Mayo

One hot chunk of melting asphalt, this block
roped off between the Phoenix Hilton
and the Museum of Science. One night unsnapped
to celebrate el Día de Independencia, Cinco de Mayo,

who cares por qué, time to party, la gente
packed tight as candies in las piñatas,
streetgangers riding low, ese, vato,
clean prom kids movin on, careful
not to sit in rented threads.

Xicanindio setting up, centerstage—
the cowbell's rich *donk!*
calls in the congas—
Jambo's palms stroke the taut skins
between kisses hello to las hijas.

Los viejitos turn las cumbias, spinning
twirled beer bottles, one leg between stockinged thighs,
tight skirt riding up, Carmen's hair
blue in the false light, the cuíca moaning
lover, Zarco milking the groaning skin,
sweet muscles, everyone's naked, especially
those with clothes on, like that woman lit up
aquí, on the corner, dancing alone, her white
strapless barely hanging on, white skirt
whispering around her calves, then rising
higher, hija, as she whirls, fireworks
breaking the sky, focusing la fiesta
upside down on the retina
of the museum's walk-in eye,
y el borracho staggers to pee in the fountain,
throws a star, and a rock falls.

The Waitress's Kid

Before you left for the Lucky Strike
I ironed your outfit—straight black
indestructible skirt, low-cut ruffles
on the K-Mart blouse. I hated

the chore as you must have the job—
toting beer to the leagues, Al Ball's
Chevron, Addressograph-Multigraph.
Once, I made you late. You came

when I called, and held me,
fought for me against some pure
and adolescent pain. Most nights
we couldn't afford it.

You'd bring home the best
of a bad lot to dance till they fell,
the crashing bodies payment
against some larger debt.

I'd yell, then cry most school nights
till exhaustion tucked you in.
But one night my anger rose past
double-edged blades in the back bathroom,

and I uncapped the little white tube
free from the Avon Lady, Furious Passion,
my color, not yours, and wrote in virgin lipstick
three words on the mirror, then opened the window

and left. You held your lipstick smack
against your mouth, one wide pull
in each direction. You'd smear your lips
against each other, then kiss

a square of toilet paper, leaving always
surprised, a mouth. Under the oleanders
behind the public pool I waited
for you to miss me. I knew you would yell

I know you can hear me just like you used to
when I was little and you said stay
within hollering distance or else, and you did
yell *I know you can*

hear me, but I heard in your voice how much
you did not know. When you left, desperate,
to wake up my friends, I walked home up the arroyo,
sure the punishment would be swift.

The Garden of Earthly Delights: Detail, Tucson

That summer, we swiped chunks of two-by-four
heaped by the cracking slabs
poured for new houses
exactly like ours, more families settling
for the exact same carport, asphalt
so soft in August our kickstands
sank in, left pedals
digging their own graves
right where they fell.

Mice in the dog chow,
crankcase oil dripped
on the crisp deformed
larkspur, the few
clutching petals
hardy and doomed.

We traced petroglyphs
in the crusty manure.

Dad's '64 Harley, cherried.
This was before the Big One,
before Mom unjammed the junk drawer,
dug out the split-handled
ball peen hammer and sank the rounded end
with cool precision tank tank tank
across the sexy
paint, till we could have set up
Chinese checkers.

Before, when the square gray barbecue
still had wheels. We heaved it
over the lip of the patio to wait
forever for the fire to burn down.

That Sunday, she came to the sliding door
just as Dad touched the match
to the fluid-soaked briquets—
                    whoosh and flare—
her face rippled and huge under glass.

Glass Rattlesnakes & the Three Incomparable Daughters of Marisol

That night the clouds gathered in packs,
Stray dogs snapping, rolling in dirt.
Mimosas bent, gossiping, to the ground.

When her breathing came heavy,
Marisol moaned for her daughters.
The room was bare, except for a bowl
Filled with plain dirt, the kind
Growling outside anyone's window.

> *I had hoped to do better*
> *But this is all I have to leave you—*
> *One scoop each of common soil.*

> *Take it now, and choose*
> *Which life you'll let it give you.*

When the last words escaped her, slowly
Marisol opened her eyes on each of her daughters.
She felt a smooth coil loosen,
Releasing her heart.
Another slid down her spine,
Riding for pleasure that spiral
Waxed banister. The third was stingy,
Its rattles strongest, the third
Held on till she turned clay,
And only then gave up
Its corkscrew hold on her sex.

So it was that death came to her,
A simple woman who left nothing
But her last breath, some plain dirt,
And her name, Marisol.
The sea took for itself the wavy part, Mar.
The sun was left without a shadow, sol.
Marisol kept only the keening vowel, *eee*
The mean prayer of her leaving.
She opened her mouth.

Three braided glass rattlesnakes
Shimmied onto her tongue, balanced there
On the dried gourds of their tails.
Marisol tipped back her head,
One last glance at blue Venus,
And the snakes flipped off, cliff divers
Hanging on mid-air gasps, swooping,
Slicing, dazzling down,
Spangling her tiles with clear
Splintered fangs.

Alegría,
The oldest daughter, reached over
And closed her mother's eyes.
With the same hand, she mashed
Fistfuls of dirt into a wide red canoe.
She kissed her sisters, then slid
Three snake slivers under her sandal strap.
The moon pulled her canoe downstream
Past the oil slick of the estuary,
Past the what-if, what-if frog echoes,
Into the wallow of the Three Crocodiles.
She fed each beast a chunk of glass,
And the glass lit up the leathery skins,
Shining through the seams. So it was
That each part of her could see
Where it was going, through the jaws'
Gateways, deep into the tails' jungles,
Every part of her could see
The whole time they devoured her.

Tristeza,
The middle daughter, combed her mother's hair
And arranged the chilling limbs to resemble
A gentle mother, napping. Then she patted
A thick quilt from her share of the soil,

Spread it in honor over her mother.
The quilt was a comfort, but didn't quite
Cover her cold left foot. Each stitch
Sprouted fruit trees—peaches, apricots,
Ruddy nectarines. Her orchard without fail
Gave back a harvest large as the appetite
Of the woman rumored to sleep under the mountain,
The restless one whose turning split the fields
And swallowed plowing farmers, their horses, their swearing.
Tristeza set up a stand at the edge of the highway,
A wooden ramada by the busy crossroads.
People stopped, asked her permission to
Glean the ripe hangers-on. They bit—teeth piercing
The downy skins, juices swimming across their tongues.
They ate in the cool shadows of the strange toes
Of rock stranded at the edge of the grove.
Tristeza fed them. They asked for more.

  Deseo,
The baby, clamped the earth tight
And would not let go. She spit on her fist
And a jaguar was born. She fed it
Hot goat's milk, scratched its forever itching
Back. The jaguar began at her ankles,
Licked her calves, she wanted more,
Licked until she begged in Portuguese.
That jaguar would not do everything she wanted.
All night Deseo climbed the staircases of tequila,
No more, panting, *end here, steps, no more.*
She reached the top landing, the one with carpets
Playing up to the blue wall, carpets
Sagging over the trapdoor. Glass eyes. Sharp pupils.
The jaguar crouched beneath her skirt.
When she touched herself, anthills!
Anthills erupted everywhere she touched herself.

Taproots

Quite suddenly
    in the Apostles' River Valley
      the acacias flower.

Their taproots throb,
    touching secret waters
      under sand so hot

even vultures suffer. Up one trunk
    the honey badger turns his head
      tooth-grip and claw-lifting living

shakes of bark, burrowing
    after the skink underneath.
      Cradling the lizard

across the pads of one paw,
    the badger regards her, noses
      her transparent belly.

The skink lies quite still,
    playing dead, her lungs fluttering
      like leftover wings

too small to lift more than the chest,
    too delicate to admit
      that the graceful curve

insinuating itself inside
    her torso matches the curve
      of the badger's nail.

Turned Wood

The thinnest vessels let through light,
tulipwood, bare rubbed mahogany.
For a bedstead or a tabletop,
the maker passed over this thick knot—

spalted sugar maple, its jagged
interruption of space turned
so intricately every hole hollowed
by water or worm, every deformity

contains its own grace. Ebony
butterflies retract split sides of the great
acacia plate. The walking bowl
two-steps, slicing twice:

shape and stripe—zebrawood.
Rabbits gnaw the lilac stem,
finches eat the fruit. Two hands
turn wood, rich woodsmell rising.

Blue Apples

Grandfather chose a name—
Lan Ping—

and laid out clean
bands of cloth

while she waded
ankle-deep

in yellow mud. When he called,
her hair swung

over melonshells, a white boat,
clay horses, one shoe.

This high-necked dress
attended her, her thighs whispering

so privately she dared not
look up. A drizzle—

blue windowbeads chattering
over the organized wrongdoing

of the fuchsia
sweating on her nightstand.

He tightened thick bandages
toe to heel

and turned from her stare.
Taught her to paint not the leaves

but the spaces
between the leaves.

Pomegranates

San Diego, 1944

Once, as a girl, she pulled down
pomegranates, ruddy and overripe,

their dry bells sounding no warning.
A sharp rock between her thighs

broke into each bulb, the thick seed
quickening her tongue. She swallowed

more than once, but could not
in this way finish the fruit.

Too much, always, when the ripe time
returns to us sticky—

her friends gathered and together
they shattered the tidy pyramid,

emptied the shells onto a long tongue
of oilcloth lapping across the back lawn.

Then one by one the uninitiated ran
wonderfully ashamed, and pressed

each new chest chest-first,
slishing barely on the blushing seed—

they kept on till the seed dried,
then rinsed off, convinced

now they knew lust,
its moment of extravagance

its secrets
wasteful enough to keep.

Snapping Turtles

At the end of Bald Cypress Trail, wooden railings.
Beyond those, the swamp, deepening
in wide hollows between loblolly pines.

Three turtles sunning, two on a log
long downed, one alone on a half-jagged
stump.

They enter the air shining,
newly-made and still gleaming, and stay out
till the luster fades utterly.

Citizens of both worlds, the hot raucous one
full of light, the muddier calm and quiet
one. Struggling out, plopping in—

they practice this ritual, again and again.

Taking a Shower with Two Girls

On one, jaguar's fur
spiked lightly wet
waiting to be licked.

On the other, the brown crease
along a tongue
of magnolia

released from its stem.
In this place, the laughter's
no more naked than the water.

I let myself be
the water.

Genealogies

Let us ask our mothers'
maiden names and discover
blue finch, cypress knee,
Spanish moss, large mouth
bass. Let us ask our fathers'
first lives, inventions, and find
beach grass, bunch grass, seawort,
sea oats. Listen—the black skimmer
tilts his narrow wing and swoops
far down, his open beak straining
the Chesapeake, swallowing whole
the light-dazzled fingerlings.

III

A man in Anatuvuk Pass, in response to a question about what he did when he visited a new place, said to me, "I listen."

—Barry Lopez, *Arctic Dreams*

The Circle of Totems

At Saxman, the totems slash down
through the mist, anchor themselves
deep in the Ketchikan muskeg
with one massive stomp
of each flat foot.
The ground, the people,
shiver, and look up.
                    The totems have chosen
this place, where alder and hemlock
crowd so thick a horse can't pass through
so tight the thick-skinned she-bear
swiping at salmonberries
must shove her cubs with the backside
of one blunt-clawed paw.
                    The totems have chosen
this rock, where chum and sockeye
whip upstream in a creek crammed full—
more fish than water—a creek where
eagles and ravens squawk, both clans
gorging themselves against the lean times,
freshening mouths lately filled
by unread entrails
from the canneries' pilings.
                    The lowest mouth
on one tall pole clamps down on the wrist
of an anguished boy. He heads out on a morning
that's spitting at him, a fine drizzle
beading his eyelashes. Weaves down
at the lowest tide to hunt devilfish,
feeling already the slick circles against his tongue.
Chewy arms for seconds
coil in the cast iron stewpot.
He can tell from the sky
this will be a good day
for devilfish.

From the surface, bayside,
his eyes show him only himself,
wavering, squinting, hanging out
on a snag at the water's edge.
One branch cracks loose, so he
pokes around, jabbing into the mouths of stone
even this low tide covers. The branch
sings a thuck and scraping song,
hard bark against hard rock,
till the boy's arms grow heavy.
His stomach sings too now, an empty song,
and he sees in his mind the hand
of his mother, patting his shoulder,
loving him even when he brings her
nothing. He wades knee-high.

At first, it's the same story—
wood against stone under a loosening sky—
but on the third try, something
throws back his stick, a soft spitting out
of its splintering. Devilfish!
He reaches right down to grab its arm,
reaches back and down so he's bent
breathing hard, reaches far in,
fingers stretched and tickling—

    Then the whole world
                     bites down!

For a moment he thinks this red-black cloud
is ink, squirted across his face
by the struggling one.

Only later does he claim it as pain,
his arm stuck in the frozen-hinged maw
of this stone-beast his fist and feet can't hurt.
He yanks and jimmies, tries relaxing
but feels only the distant spreading of his bones
traveling through his opening flesh.

　　　　When he remembers to breathe,
he takes the deepest breath he can remember.
As soon as it's in, it wants out,
forces itself as a rippling long scream
up the hillside, through rocks and thickets,
past the work sheds where two Tlingit carpenters
are jacking up the roof of the carver's barn.
That scream clears the fog and brings the people,
his whole village, down.
　　　　　　　　　　　　The strongest men
try with iron bars to break the face
of the great rock oyster.
But the water's coming home, as it does.
Up to his hips, his waist,
the boy knows this is his day,
straightens himself as much as he can.
He looks at his people,
at the eagle,
the raven,
the beaver-tail clan.
The water around his chest
lifts him a little, and he sings
his own song, a song of red and black,
of salmon shimmering in their buttons,
a song of fur buried under a stake
at the beach, so sand and water
can scrub it white, white fur
his mother will sew at the edges
of new moccasins,

the ones he will wear a long time
without any holes wearing through.

His people remember the song,
though it passed through the air
only once. They sing it
for the master carver who sharpens
his chisels and sets to work,
freeing the boy's spirit
from a five-ton trunk of cedar.
The carver's tools chant—

    Remember, remember, remember.
    Prepare. Prepare. Prepare.

Where Mountains Have No Names

Moving water melts the glacier
from the inside out. We listen,
trace its widening along the flatland.

A yearling moose strips new bark
off low-hanging birch, thrashes
and stomps knee-deep in the stream.

Vast, bountiful, unforgiving—
the ways of water's being.

Blue Ridge Reservoir

So few people
pass this way
the watersnake tilts
his head, but doesn't
bolt.

Along Blue Ridge
our sunstroked Eagle
floats, her brim scorching
unrested elbows, her sloping basin
mud-cool to bare toes.

The inobtrusive shush
of canoe paddles
interrupts the surface
just for a moment, and with reason.

Only at a certain slant
can light show twice
what's here—carrying on
as if what's below
powdered water
snags and silt
toeholds breathing in rock

as if what we take on faith,
accept without question,
or give up to mystery—
all the underworld, undisturbed,
fertile in its brooding,

simply turns the world we touch
back on itself.

Lost Watch

Buried under ash and eggplant
a woman's gold watch
marks off the blue wilderness
left to her.

The clasp let go &
without even gravity
to betray it,
her watch slipped away

a stray star passing.
Inside, its circles muster
the gears of infinity,
the crystal visions of desire.

Frost seals in
a study in blue and white:
two milk-hands groping
for a privacy

that skates through solitude,
ten blue ovals nearly frozen,
nails breaking past
crust on new powder.

Hour hand, minute hand,
keeping track of her steps,
back to the clothesline,
retracing the fence.

October, Snow

Quiet snow takes on
the shape of the black branch
that's taking on snow.

This low
along the horizon
the sun

seems hurt,
glazes one birch in last light.
First ice

across the Chena edges out
until two sharpnesses
wound each other into binding.

Dry snow gives way
to the slightest urgings. One black seed
ticks through the crust.

First Winter: Joy

Yesterday at ten below
we tried to hang a birdfeeder
to the lowest strong branch
of the birch outside the big window.

I held the little redwood
chalet by one eave.
He bent, and tucked his head
between my thighs, lifted me

laughing high enough to loop
blue filaments of fishing leader
into crooks in the bark.
Spilt seed nestled in his curls.

I tied one knot. By then,
my earlobes had stopped hurting.
The fingers in my gloves
weren't taking orders.

So I trussed it up
best I could, and we
ran, remembering why kids run
everywhere, back inside.

This morning, the seed
has all drained away,
a perfect heap in the snow,
the glass house
dangling by one corner.

Bush Navigator: The Last Morning of Hands

Dieter bit his sealskin mitts, and pulled.
Wind made ice in his knucklebones.

His maps spiraled out
into the copter's bubble—
he rolled them backwards
so they might lie flat.

Sheer as a salmon's eyelid
a windshear slashed
the jagged air,
whipped their bubble sideways
to the surface—
hacking blades stuttered
sparking against granite
three quarters up
a mountainside nobody owned.

The place had no name.
This offended him.

The last thing his hands felt
was the faint strum
of Leonid's pulse
quieting. One by one
he counted off his fingers
as the frost pointed out
uncharted boundaries, elevations, depths—
each graphic thing he would never touch.

The Inupiat Christmas Pageant

Under the red Korean banner
spanning the space above the altar
of the Episcopal Church
downtown in Fairbanks,
from way out in the bush
or just up from Two Street,
the faithful and the unfaithful gather.

The choir, like most choirs,
all women. Lining up to march in,
bright cotton calf-length
hooded dresses, silent
caribou foot coverings.

Flat drums, firm beat,
knee bends, grass fans.

Joseph's ermine
and squirrel tail coat,
ruff of hollow wolverine.

Hunters, not shepherds, searching
the night sky, tracing
string webs and stars
to mark a way
across sea ice.

Gifts of the whale captains:
a sealskin, mukluks,
tiny parka for the fur-swaddled child.

Glottal stopped, chopped
"Adeste Fidelis."

Koolaid, Oreos, and
bread born of lowbush cranberries.
Slices of raw turnip
dipped in seal oil.

Kiernan's jovial yank
breaks his mama's string
of blue beads—
we kneel to retrieve them—
shiny Siamese cats' eyes
skipping over dust
under straightbacked pews.

He laughs out loud,
this child conceived
when a sterile syringe let go
the milky rush and one
of millions whipped through
selfless whiteness to unite
with a small orb
traveling imperceptibly
through the lightless season.

About the Author

Peggy Shumaker was born in La Mesa, California, in 1952. She grew up in Tucson, Arizona, and received her B.A. and M.F.A. from the University of Arizona. From 1979 to 1985 she served as a writer-in-residence for the Arizona Commission on the Arts. Her first book of poems, *Esperanza's Hair,* was published in 1985. Director of the Writing Program at Old Dominion University, she lives in Norfolk, Virginia.